Twenty-One Days of *Falling In Love* with LUPUS

Published By:
Jasher Press & Co.
New Bern, NC 28561
Interior & Cover PDS

Copyright© 2018

ISBN: **978-1984233561**

All rights reserved. Except for brief excerpts used in reviews, no portion of this work may be reproduced or published without expressed written permission from the author or the author's agent.

First Edition
Printed and bound in the United States of America

Twenty-One Days of Falling In Love with Lupus

Table of Contents

- Dedication 7
- Introduction 9
- Day 1 17
- Day 2 21
- Day 3 23
- Day 4 25
- Day 5 27
- Day 6 29
- Day 7 31
- Day 8 33
- Day 9 35
- Day 10 37
- Day 11 39
- Day 12 41
- Day 13 43
- Day 14 47
- Day 15 51
- Day 16 55
- Day 17 57
- Day 18 59
- Day 19 61
- Day 20 63
- Day 21 65
- Conclusion Of The Matter 67
- Acknowledgments 69

DEDICATION

With love, I dedicate this book to all Lupus survivors and fallen Lupus patients that battles or has battled this deadly disease.

Special Recognition:

Marsha Meadows

Faye Koonce

I also dedicate this book to my hometown Trenton, North Carolina

With Love.

INTRODUCTION

I grew up the small town of Trenton, North Carolina. In this town, there is one stop light, two stores, two gas stations, and three restaurants. There are many farms, corn fields, and cotton fields. There are not many people, but it's a place I'm proud to call home. Growing up in Trenton, I didn't have many opportunities like most children in the city, but I still felt like I had everything I needed.

I was raised in a two parent household with two other siblings. Many would say I was the problem child, but I would say I was just strong-minded. My sisters and I were super spoiled and loved by my two parents, grandparents, and great-grandparents. It was a blessing to have both parents in the same household and all of my grandparents in my life. I wouldn't have traded this for the world. The best thing about having my grandparents in my life was being able to really experience the country life while my parents were away making a living for me. When I visited my Mema's house, I knew I was going to receive a good country meal with chicken and rice, fried rabbit, or fresh eggs from the chicken cope. I spent most of my days getting off the bus at her house, or as we call it today "41 East".

If I went to my great-grandmother's house, or "Mother" as we called her, I knew I would be able to receive a peanut butter and jelly sandwich--and I better not cut off the edges! Mother stayed on Backstreet. That's where I met most of my childhood friends playing hot potato, riding bikes, hide-and-seek, and red rover. I can still feel the sand spurs in my legs, see the grass stains on my clothes, and see the smiles on my childhood friend's faces as we approached each other walking through our yards.

The last place where I was super spoiled was GranGran and Grandaddy's house. They both spoiled me and my sisters rotten. We had endless amounts of food and candy. This was my weekend get-away when my parents needed a break or went out of town. I loved the smell of the pancakes, the sound of Uncle Leon coming in at three in the morning, or even the smell of my granddaddy's cigars.

Overall, my experience in school was kind of rough. It was a rocky road in elementary and middle school. I stayed in the principal's office and I was suspended a few times. Throughout most of elementary and middle school, I was teased because of a speech problem. Many students would copy me as I walked by in the hallways or pretended to be my friend just to make cruel jokes about me. This made it difficult to focus in school. I did not do well on many assignments and I even started to lash out on my parents and teachers. I felt unwanted, like I did not belong.

I remember one of the biggest breaking points was when a group of females spit in my food when I got up to get a napkin. I had no knowledge of them doing this until I ate the whole meal. I recall going to mother, crying and asking her, "Mommy, will they ever stop?" It was safe to say that at this point in life, I despised school.

In 2009, I finally reached high school, attending Jones Senior High School. This was a new start for me. I had a great friend that I called "Crab Cakes." She basically adopted me, at least that's what it felt like. I'd never had that type of friendship before. I was introduced to all of the upperclassmen because she was a junior. I no longer had to worry about the classmates that came to high school at the same time as me. Things were finally starting to look up for me. I was playing sports, making honor roll, and I even started to feel love for the first time. One day, as I was walking down the wing, a popular basketball player stopped me. He said, "Aye, freshman! Can I get your number?" I knew I would love him as soon as I turned around--and I did. I fell and I fell fast. I remember it like it was yesterday. I called him "My Street Kid." Soon, all of my happiness began to fade away again. The upperclassmen graduated. I lost my friend and my first love moved away to his fathers in Alabama.

So, I was back with my classmates, feeling lonely without dependable friends. That emptiness began to reappear, but this time it was different. I remained focused. It was senior year and I had to graduate and get accepted to a four year university. My senior year, I had no idea that God was going to send me a lifetime friend and that I would one day call her my best Friend. I think God knew that I needed her. She kept me encouraged and supported me even when I failed. In 2013, I did not get accepted to a university until the first week of June. As you can imagine,

I was infuriated. Everyone else had already received their acceptance letters. But when I got that letter, I realized God did not forget about me. I was accepted to Elizabeth City State University, the "Home Of The Mighty Vikings." I couldn't have been happier for the simple fact that Elizabeth City State University was my first choice. I knew as soon as I reached the campus that this University is where I was destined to be.

Of course, attending Elizabeth City State University was a grand experience. I met awesome people from all backgrounds, professors that cared, and most of all--it felt like home. It was small, full of love and diversity. While I was in college, I had four friends that were worthy of having the title "friend." They were called E, Rae Bae, Rae, and Bash. These were the crazy nicknames we called each other. Every time we called each other's names, the laughter in our voices already told the stories before we said another word. The type friendship we had was full of love, laughter, and joy. I was honored to have them in my life.

On the other hand, during my sophomore year of college I started to have female issues. I either had a very heavy cycle or I just wouldn't have one at all. I went to see a gynecologist and the doctor tested my blood work. The doctor said I tested positive for diabetes. I started taking a medicine called Metformin to help keep me from being full-blown diabetic. As time passed on, I started to have pain in my lower legs that felt like numbness or a tingling sensation. Many people will tell you this is normal for a person who is diabetic. The pain started to get unbearable, so I was referred to a rheumatologist. They took my blood work and called me back a couple of days later. The rheumatologist informed me that I was missed diagnosed. I was not a diabetic, but I did test positive for a disease called Lupus.

Lupus is a chronic inflammatory disease that occurs when your body's immune system attacks your own tissues and organs. Inflammation caused by Lupus can affect many different body systems, including your joints, skin, kidneys, blood cells, brain, heart and lungs. This disease mainly affected my joints and skin such as my fingers, legs, arms, and toes. I have rashes, hair loss, fatigue, numbness in my limbs, and flare ups. When I received this phone call, I didn't know that my whole life would change. It never occurred to me that I would wake up one day and never get better.

DAY 1

I called my mother to tell her the news that I just received from the doctor, telling her that I tested positive for lupus. As the phone was ringing, I could feel myself going numb. When she answered the phone, I couldn't figure out exactly how to tell her. So, I started off by saying, "Mommy, the doctor called." After I told her the news, she insisted that she and Mema came to visit. Half of me wanted them to come and the other half didn't. I did not want them to see me cry or see that I was really not okay. When they finally arrived, I kept it together well. My mother kept asking me if I was okay and I would tell her that I was. Truthfully, I did not know what to say. My sisters and father eventually called to check on me. They gave me words of encouragement, but really and truly, I don't think they knew what to say either.

In the meantime, I was still living on campus in the Suites. My close friend Rae was living down the hall from me, as well as a guy I called JuneJune who seemed to be interested in me. JuneJune called me to come up to his room so we could talk. I really did not feel like talking, but I kept a smile on my face and continued to act normal. I felt like a balloon with too much air inside, waiting to pop. When I did finally talk to him, I fell into shambles.

In that moment, I just needed someone to be there. He stared at me like a bad fungus; he had so much confusion on his face. I could not take how he was looking at me, so I buried my face into his shoulder thinking he would comfort me--but he didn't. I left the room in hurry, I just had to get away. I didn't understand why he didn't console me! By the time I reached my room, Rae was on my bed. My roommate was a mutual friend of ours. I jumped on the bed and didn't say a word. I could feel my chest tighten and my heart breaking like glass. I just laid there. Rae didn't say a word, but she wrapped her arms around me and held me while I cried. I guess that's what friends are for because she had no idea how much I needed that good cry.

Thank you, Rae.

"Not everybody has to me love, and that's okay."

DAY 2

Why did I wake up feeling like someone had beaten my heart to death? By the time I finally got out of bed and my feet touched the floor, I felt like the life had been sucked out of me. In that moment, I could feel the depression start to sink in.

However, I did my normal routine. I got dressed for class and painted this smile on my face. I had to act normal because I didn't want anybody asking me questions like, "Are you okay?" So that's exactly what I did. I went about my day like always. I saw Rae and she didn't say much, but that was okay. After all, what do you say to your friend that has been diagnosed with a disease? I understood the awkwardness that was in the room.

Finally, as the day progressed, I made it back to my room. I had a roommate and I couldn't let her see that I was starting to fall apart as the day came to an end. While I was taking my nightly shower, I looked in the mirror and I asked God, "Why me?" I slowly fell down by the sink, crawled into this little ball, and cried. I just couldn't seem to keep it together any longer. In that moment, God and I needed to have a conversation. The anger that I felt towards him was unthinkable. He needed to help me understand. He knew that I battled depression at a young age, that I was bullied, and that nothing has really been "easy breezy" for me. So God, why me? I just couldn't handle the thought of this disease. How will I make it through college if I can't sleep at night because I'm in pain? After a while, I realized that God is mute and I wouldn't get any answers. I would just have to deal with it and find my own way.

"God is mute for a reason, which makes him the best listener."

DAY 3

I did not sleep that night. My toes felt numb and my legs felt like needles had been stabbing me over and over. I did not pray either because I still haven't figured a way to speak to God without being so livid. I'm sure God was as disappointed in me as I was with Him in that moment.

That day, a band girl in my dorm asked me to sew in her weave for the game the next day. I said yes because I didn't have anything else to do. When she entered my room, she brought me the hair. The hair was in shambles because it has been fairly used. She gave me specific directions on how she wanted it to look. Of course, I tried to accommodate her as best as possible, but as I was doing her hair my legs started to ache. My knees started to feel weak, as if I would collapse at any second. I tried to be as discrete as possible, trying not to show her that I was in pain.

I finished her sew-in and I got ready to curl her hair. When I finished, she looked in the mirror and said, "Messy, my curls are not tight of enough." I looked puzzled because I was tired, my legs hurt, and I wasn't a beautician. I tried to keep calm and recoil her hair, but I assumed that it was still not how she wanted it. After I finished, she grabbed her things and left without a thank you. In that very moment, I felt really unappreciated. I did her hair for free and she had no idea how much pain I was in while standing. I was trying to do her a favor and she wasn't appreciative at all. Some people will never know the things that a total stranger will go through just to accommodate you.

"It's okay to say NO."

DAY 4

I had just recently had a doctor's appointment and there was no good news at all. I was now taking eight pills, and one of them made me feel sick. I had to call out of work, because standing was just unbearable.

If I knew that I was going to wake up to my manager fussing me out for the simple fact that I was sick, I would have never woken up. I called my mommy to inform her of my work situation. She called my manager to handle the issue and to let her know about my situation. I'm so grateful for my mother.

Later I received a text message saying that I called out of work because I had a sexually transmitted disease.

The lack of knowledge about what Lupus is began a rumor that wasn't even true.

However, I knew social media would get my message out quickly. I logged into Facebook and told the world about my disease called lupus. I figured that trying to hide it for months was enough. After I pressed that post button, I felt a little relieved. In that moment, I no longer cared what people thought about my sickness. I figured that I shouldn't worry about something others don't understand.

"I owe myself so many apologies."

DAY 5

The phone rang off the hook as I pondered what all the fuss was about. My family sent text messages and phone calls, asking me if I had seen my best friend's Facebook post. All I could think was, "Who is my best friend trying to beat up now?" I logged into my Facebook to see that she had gotten a Lupus tattoo on her back. It was a purple Lupus ribbon with my name on it. My heart melted over and over again. Tears wouldn't stop falling from my face. I don't think she understood what that meant to me. If she only knew that I thought about giving up every day. If she only knew that I feared death, loneliness, and heartbreak every day because of this disease.

If my best friend only knew that she gave me the desire to live, all because of that tattoo.

Thank you, Best Friend.

"My Best friend is my most important asset."

DAY 6

Who created these medications? They suck! My hair was falling out, I couldn't eat without throwing up, and why didn't the doctor tell me that it would worsen my depression? I woke up before class to take my medication and threw it up before I could walk out the door. That's not even the embarrassing part. The embarrassing part was that someone saw me throwing up and asked if I was pregnant. But here's the kicker, they don't know that it's hard to have a child when you have Lupus. It's hard to decide which one broke my heart more, throwing up constantly or not being able to have my own child one day.

Throughout that day, things only got worse. My family and I went out to eat. As I was eating, I started to feel sick and had the urge to throw up. I ran to the bathroom, knowing I probably looked insane running through a restaurant. As soon as I reached the bathroom, I got sick. While I was throwing up, I could feel the tears fall down my face. Again, God, why me?

Before I could leave the bathroom, my oldest sister came to console me. I was glad that she came to check on me. I wonder if my sister knows how much it means to me that she always supports me and has my back.

"I am not my sister's keeper; I am my sister."

DAY 7

I was now a statistic. I was sure that where I was headed, I would still be alone. I was overwhelmed with grief and I expected to find sympathy when I got here. I just found more people like me, full of grief, fear, and heartbreak. People like me who were wounded warriors with rashes, patchy hair, slit wrists, and mouth sores. They may as well have given me a number and sat me in a category called "Fragile Lupus Patients".

That day, I felt like I should have just died. I wished that I would've stayed home. I remember how anxious I was to meet people like me. I did not know that when I entered the room, I would be looking at myself in the mirror. Each person told the same story of having miscarriages, headaches, unbearable pain. As they told their stories I felt my heart shatter more and more. It kind of felt like I was drowning and I needed someone to save me, but they didn't. I just died over and over again as each person told their story. Where was the support that I need? This was not what I came for. It felt more like I was seeing a future teller who was telling me my future. I wanted this to bring me happiness and to make me feel hopeful.

They spoke about how our life expectancy could range from 15 to 45. They said that we should avoid stress, sunlight, eat right, and exercise. This bullshit. I'm just another statistic.

"The secret to being happy is to know that you are the secret"

DAY 8

I've been told that I am a beautiful person. From my skin to my eyes, and even my physique. Apparently I don't see what others see. When I look at myself, I see the long weave I have in my hair to cover up my sores and hair loss caused by the side effects of my medication. When I look down at my body, I see the weight that I've gained in my stomach and thighs. I think about how I'll never be a size five again, or how I will never be able to wear that crop-top again like my sisters and friends. These steroids are supposed to make me feel better, and internally they do, but physically I feel like I look horrible. I use makeup everyday to cover the bags under my eyes and my swollen face. I even cover up my rashes just to keep people from asking about my awful disease. Keeping my toes and nails done is the only thing that keeps me going. I know it may seem weird, but that brings me so much life.

Many of my friends often ask me why I wear makeup, lashes, a weave, and nails. They don't realize that every piece of me feels like I need these things. They keep me together, not to just to make me attractive to others, but so I can feel attractive myself. I'm going through a trial were my whole life is falling apart. I have too many changes in my body and I don't know to deal with it, so I cover it up. I wish they would just allow me to let go when I'm ready, but for now these material things are the only things keeping me together.

"Please let me keep my paint brush with me until I learn to love me too."

DAY 9

You think you understand, and I know you think you do.

But hearing you speak, you don't even have a clue. I know you're trying to help me, but your help is useless if you don't understand.

I told you I didn't sleep well last night and you say "Me too." I told you my body aches from the cold, you say "Wear more clothes." You ask me to go out. I tell you I don't feel good. Then you ask why do I always cancel plans on you.

You tell me that I'm not the same person who can stay up late and still go to work the next day. You say I have changed. I know to you it doesn't appear that I am sick, but I really am. This is a real battle that I face daily. If you really knew me, you would know this isn't my fault. I didn't plan this to be a part of my life.

There isn't much that you can do. I just need for you to understand and listen to me. Don't try to tell me how I should feel. Just listen. Take some time and learn what I'm actually going through. Then you will see my pain.

Each day is a different battle that I fight. The only thing that is steady is my failing immune system. If you want to help me, educate yourself on my disease before you tell me what you think.

Show me that you believe me. Show me that I don't need proof of my scars. Tell me it is okay to be different and boring. Don't refuse to see me. This is who I am now. I cannot hide who I am, just remember through it all--I'm still me.

"Everyone is not going to understand your experience, be patient and help them understand to."

DAY 10

If it wasn't for Facebook, I swear I wouldn't keep in contact with any of my classmates. A classmate that has the same name as me reached out to me. She wrote me and said that life was too short and how she heard that I was sick. She is someone that I have cared for over the years, but we just couldn't get this friendship thing right. My experience with her throughout the years made me feel like she could only be my friend behind closed doors. Which is truly okay, because I stopped caring about friends years ago. Her message didn't mean anything to me, just like the other 500 messages that I had received. I know so many people think it's the thought that counts, but the thought doesn't count if it isn't genuine.

In spite of all the things I have been through with my classmates, I forgive them. But I will not allow them to reenter my life as I am battling Lupus. I just would hate to put my trust in someone that I thought cared for me and really doesn't. You do know that you can die from a broken heart right? From now on, I am looking out for me.

"Life is about who you loved and who you hurt."

DAY 11

If you see me rotating my arms randomly, it's because it feels like they are numb or losing circulation.

If you call me and cannot hear me, it is because the phone is on speaker phone because holding the phone is a hard task for me.

If you're riding with me and I put the car in park at a red light, it's because my legs are killing me and holding the break down is difficult.

If you invite me to a club or event and I don't attend. Please don't be mad with me. It's because if the location does not have chairs, standing up is hard for me.

If you catch me staring out into space or maybe I just don't seem okay, it's because I'm thinking about this journey that I'm facing.

If you text me or call me and I don't reply, please don't be angry with me. It was probably a hard day for me.

If you don't hear from me, please understand. Recently it has been hard for me to even breathe.

If I'm not laughing or smiling, please don't question me. Sometimes, when I need a break, I put a mask on so you don't see how I really feel. But some days I can't hide it--depression is real!

"This disease isn't your fault so don't try to forgive yourself, because it's nothing to forgive"

DAY 12

I feel numb to everything. It is like I have had everything swept away--my feelings, body, hair, relationships. I really don't know God's plan for me, but half of the time I don't feel like I want to be here anymore. I'm trying to keep pushing, but my health is failing. My car was recently totaled, which put more stress on my body.

My nights have been restless because I'm up all night due to pain in my legs. What made it worse was that I had school in the morning. Some days I just feel bad and my heart feels so heavy. Sometimes it's like nothing in the world would make me smile. Feelings of being worthless, broken, and no longer feeling attractive have set in. I guess this is the depression that the bottles of my medication said to be mindful of. What makes it worse is that the relationship that I had with friends and my significant other are fading away. Most of the time I don't want to be bothered. I won't even answer their calls or text messages. I'm pushing valuable people away and for the first time and my life, I don't even care.

I even go to work and nobody even notices that I am dying right in front of their faces. They can't even see the pain that was lingering around in my eyes. My mom called and I wonder if she could hear in my voice that she was losing me slowly but surely. I wonder if God even hears me praying anymore or my silent cries during the night. For the first time in my life, I can say I'm NOT okay. I am broken and I am dying.

"It's okay, it's okay. I'm going to be okay."

DAY 13

I wake up feeling worse than I did the day before. I hit my alarm clock and turned it completely off with my mind made up--I wasn't going to class today. I was determined to make my bed, but even that determination fails sometimes. As I tried to make my bed, I fell to the floor, wrapped myself in my covers, and just laid there. The tears started to fall and they just wouldn't stop falling. Not only am I in a bad place physically, but mentally too. The feelings of brokenness and lifelessness have taken over my mind. This little voice in my head is telling me God isn't hearing my cry and that this fight is useless.

I decided to text my sister to let her know I'm done with fighting. I just can't do this anymore. I'm so tired. As I sent the text message it said...

Me: Dee, I'm tired. I cannot do this anymore.

I'm her keeper: What's wrong, Dessa?

Me: I don't want to be here anymore.

I'm her keeper: What do you need? Do you need some money?

Me: No, I'm okay.

  She responded and called too many times to name. I didn't respond. I went to the kitchen, grabbed the sharpest knife I could find, and walked in the bedroom. I laid on the floor because I was about to cut my wrist. I knew this was the quickest way if I put my hands over my head. As soon as I grabbed the knife, my aunt busted through the door. All I could think was that my sister must have called my mom, and my mom must have called my aunt. My mom knew that she had a key to my apartment. In a hurry, I rushed to get off of the floor and wipe my tears, but I knew she could tell something was wrong. When I saw her face, I thought "Maybe I don't want to die." I left with her and visited my cousins. Seeing the life in those children and how they ran to me as I entered the door, I knew I wanted to live again. As strange as it sounds, I believe they gave me a little bit of life that day.

"We were born with angel wings; we just prefer to crawl through life."

DAY 14

I went back to my hometown for the weekend. The drive was smooth and the smell of the stinking air was actually gratifying. I knew that when I smelled that stinking turkey farm, I was home. For the first time in my life, I actually appreciated the sound of crickets, the fear of wild animals, and the bright stars that stretch across the sky. I'm sure they have all of these things in Virginia, but it's not same as the country.

Being home gave me that extra energy I needed. It felt like my family and hometown were the jumper cables and I was the car. They charged me back up. I really did need that trip, the endless laughs I shared with my sisters, and the food that my papa cooked. Oh, it was just what I had been longing for.

Going home takes a big toll on my body. The drive is almost four hours and it's not easy on my body at all, sitting in a car that long without stopping. As we were sitting in the family room, my arm felt like it was losing circulation. So I got up and went in my mother's room. I laid there for a while, tossing and turning. The numbness in my arm wouldn't seem to go away. The tears started to fall from my eyes, but I tried so hard to hold them back. All I could think about was how I couldn't let my family see me cry. My papa spotted me and told my momma. She came in the back room and asked me what was wrong. I tried so hard to lie and to say I was okay, but I think she read right through me. My mother is a Licensed Practical Nurse. She worked my arm in a circular motion like she does with her clients. It actually felt better. My momma told me, "Destiny, there's going to be some good days and some bad days, but you are going to be okay."

"Most people's heroes come in the form of great leaders, my hero is my mom."

DAY 15

While I was home, I attended my doctor's appointment in New Bern. I have been going to this doctor ever since I was diagnosed. I'm always nervous to go because of the news I may hear. It is never good. My loved ones often ask to go with me, but I always try to avoid them, just in case I break down. I try so hard to stay strong and I don't want them to worry about me.

As I sat on the table, my thoughts were all over the place. I knew that last time, my blood work wasn't the best. Who knows what it is now. When the doctor entered the room, he basically read the notes from the last appointment. He was speaking like he knew me or remembered my case. I started to tell him how I was feeling. I told him about how I can barely remember anything, I have no energy, and how walking is beginning to be a tough task. He gave me a quick physical, added another pill to my list, and sent me off for more blood work. I was so livid I could have spit fire. He didn't listen to me or even look up at my face to know who I was. I needed him to listen. I need him to do more. I just need him to actually be my doctor for five minutes.

As I was leaving town, I stopped by my GranGran's house to speak. As we were sitting at the table talking, she asked how I was doing and about my doctor's appointment. I said, "GranGran, that man didn't even listen to me. He just threw me some more pills." Staring into her eyes, I could feel my heart start to break. Then, the tears wouldn't stop falling. My GranGran is a God-fearing woman. She said, "Destiny, I'm praying for you. There's nothing God can't do. He's preparing you for greater. Just believe."

My GranGran believes that I'm going to be a preacher, but with everything God and I have been through, I just pray he doesn't forget about me.

"I will probably never find God, but He will find me."

DAY 16

One day I will wake up and this will all make sense. I'm going to realize that all of the prayers that I sent to God reached Him, wrapped in His tender love and mercy. I'm going to grasp that just when I thought it was over, I was actually okay. I will see that everything I went through, I was supposed to go through it. I will realize that everyone that left in my journey of battling Lupus was supposed to leave, everyone I was supposed to meet I met. I will understand that everything I thought, prayed, or spoke I did it. Every doctor's appointment I feared, I made it through. I have realized after the cursing and fussing that, because of God's love for me, I went through what I needed to go through and I'm right where I'm supposed to be.

I'm no longer feeling sorry for myself. I give in. God, you win. I'm going to think differently now. I'm going to say, "Thank you, God" even though I may be having a bad day. I'm going to love myself now. I'm always going to let others love me as well. I'll find a new doctor who listens! No more wasted tears. I'm okay. This is one time in my life I'm saying, "I'm okay" and I actually mean it.

"I'll fall short a million and one times, but it doesn't matter as long as I pick myself up at million and two."

DAY 17

It was one of my close friend's birthdays. She was turning twenty-three. We have been close since my sophomore year of college. She and I have gotten in plenty of trouble together over the years. She is someone that has taken care of me on my sickest of days. Most of the time, she makes sure I eat, rest, and even spends nights in the hospital with me.

We invited plenty of her friends over that she grew up with to hang out before we all go out. Most of us were dressed from head to toe with dresses, heels, and makeup. As we laughed, drank, and had a good time talking with one another, one of the friends she went high school with pulled me aside. She asked me why I didn't have any heels on. I kindly told her that I'm sick and having heels on when standing in the club would be difficult for me.

For the first time in my life, I was okay with being different. I'd rather look different and wear sandals, flats, or boots to the club then hurt the whole entire time, knowing I wouldn't be able to walk the next day if I wore heels.

"Lupus took my heels, but not my spirit."

DAY 18

I remember when I was growing up, I hated washing clothes. My mother would have my sisters and I wash every weekend. I hated it so much because we couldn't even go anywhere until all the clothes were washed. My sisters would wash them and I would fold them, because I would forget to go change the loads. If I forgot, my oldest sister wouldn't be too happy with me.

Now that I have moved out and I'm living on my own, I no longer have team-work to help me wash clothes. The worst part is when I try to wash clothes, standing up to sort them is difficult for me. I never thought that one day, one thing I would want the most would be to just be able to stand up and wash clothes.

Lupus is still teaching me life lessons every day, like to never take the small things for granted. Not only that, but always cherish the people around you who help you with the small things in life. Life is unpredictable, so we as individuals just need to be thankful for life's little struggles. I'm sure there's someone out in the world that can't stand or walk at all. Heck, there are people out there who don't even have legs. So instead of getting mad, I'll wash clothes a different way. I'll just sit on the floor, sort my clothes, and make a way out of no way.

"I am responsible for my day."

DAY 19

Dear Lupus,

Because of you, I live in pain when I don't deserve to. Because of you, I will never know what a regular day without medication is. I wouldn't wish this on my worst enemy, but I'm going to say thank you. I thank you because you showed me I can live through anything life could throw at me. You have taught me that it's okay to cry and that in the morning it will be just a tad bit bitter. You proved to me that I was stronger than I knew. I am now a fighter and a survivor. You showed me that God is forever faithful. I didn't like you at first, but I want to thank you. You have shown me how to love myself and I needed that more than anything.

Sincerely,

One of the many survivors

I know Lupus isn't an actual person, but I feel like Lupus needs to know how she has affected my life. I call her a she because she's a part of me now and has been for a while. I was just afraid to confront her. From this day on, I will let her know when she makes me sad, tell her my experiences, my dreams, my hopes, and my prayers. We are going through this journey together now.

"You deserve peace."

DAY 20

Having Lupus not only affects your social life, job, family, but they seem to forget to tell you it also affects your love life and sex life. Having a significant other while battling a sickness seems so selfish to me. I've never in my life wanted to be a burden to someone else. I feel like if I had a boyfriend, I would be a burden to him.

My boyfriend came down to spend time with me, which is something I enjoy. He gives me a little more life and hope. As we proceeded with our weekend, I began to feel sick and irritated. I got really light headed when we were out and about. I did not want to tell him I was feeling bad, but I figured he could tell. We were supposed to go grab a bite, but I felt so awful he insisted he take me home. Of course, I did not want to be selfish because he had not eaten all day. So I became argumentative and told him I was okay. He did not listen to me and took me back to the house. I laid down on the couch and took my meds. Eventually, I fell asleep. I woke up hours later with him sitting by my side.

Finally, I told him over and over about how I did not understand why he chose to stay home and starve while I rested. He said, "I wanted to make sure you were okay; I'll eat later". That's how I knew he really loved me. For the past few months, I was stuck on trying to figure out how you love some when their whole world is falling apart and when they are dying right in front of your eyes. Until I saw that no matter what I go through, this man is going to have my back. Now that it is love.

"Enjoy the feeling of being in love, instead of worrying about how it works."

DAY 21

Dear God,

I am giving you my pain that flows through my body and keeps me up late at night. I know I suffer because when I am in despair my faith is weary. I know I cry because I feel like you are not with me. I ask that you open my mind so I will know, open my heart so I can receive love from others, open my eyes so I can see the many blessings that cover me. Bring joy to my life and happiness to my soul, and my dear God, bring forgiveness to my heart. Amen.

"God is patient, God is kind, and God is God through it all."

CONCLUSION OF THE MATTER

The day the doctor diagnosed with me Lupus still feels like yesterday. The tone of the doctor's voice, the silence in the room, the words of a lifelong disability, no cure, and the sound of "I'm sorry" still hurts. Why do I allow myself to ponder on that day? I have stared into space many of days thinking about things my doctor forgot to mention. I would have sleepless nights. He forgot to mention the fatigue and how sometimes I would not be able to eat. Someone forgot to mention that I would never feel young again and that my immune system would be weak and possibly shut down at any time. Why didn't he mention that Lupus was messy? I wish someone would have mentioned that Lupus is expensive--the doctors, medication, and the numerous heating pads.

The doctor forgot to mention that my strength will triumph over Lupus, that my tears would create rainbows, and that my laughter would brighten up the room. How did the doctor forget to mention that I, Destiny Ward, would inspire millions and heal so many broken hearts with this paper and pen? I go to sleep eagerly every night, just to discover what the doctor forgot to mention.

"I learned that God is the answer, no matter what the question is."

ACKNOWLEDGMENTS

Writing a book is not easy. Part of the process is exhilarating, but part of it is not. Writing "Twenty-One Days of Falling in Love with Lupus" was one of the hardest tasks I have ever endured.

I was helped in very significant ways as I wrote this, and I want to deeply thank the individuals who poured words of encouragement, played a part in my day-to-day life, and even inspired me to follow my dreams with writing this. I could not have written this book without them.

Jasher Press, Demya Ward, Danielle Ward, Ashleyh Korgar, D'Aja Fulmore all added immeasurably to the editing process. Each of them were there to push me and keep me inspired through this process.

My Thanks to Jasher Press and also D'Aja Fulmore for giving me a opportunity to write this book and trusting that I had something of value in mind when I proposed this idea. It is an honor to work under your supervision and guidance.

Thanks to my parents, Richard and Elizabeth Ward, for giving me all the tools I needed to get through life. I realize when I wrote this book, I already had everything I needed because of them.

Thanks as well to Tanisha Dunn, Ashleyh Korgar, Jamar Suiter, Brittany Ward, Ieshia Williams, Desirae Smith, and Andrew Bryant for the bonds and treasures of friendships.

Thank you to the many people who were so kind to me during the days I felt like Lupus was taking over my life. The support, love, and generosity shown to me are gifts that I may never be able to return. Hopefully, this book has shown you that even you can grow in twenty-one days.

Thank you to everyone who read my book, came to my events, or helped me along the way. I hold each of you close to my heart and pray for you more than I pray for myself--and those are not just words.

Twenty-One Days of Falling In Love with Lupus

About the Author

Destiny Ward was diagnosed with Lupus in the year of 2014. She is now an author, speaker, and activist for Lupus.

Her love for inspiring other has lead her to being a Mental Health Counselor to help people nationwide who battles diseases, depression, and suicidal thoughts.

She truly believes that everyone deserve a glimpse of heaven.

Contact:

Facebook: DestinyWard

Email: 21daysofFILWF@Gmail.com

Twenty-one Days of Falling In Love With Lupus

Printed in Great Britain
by Amazon